NO ONE'S LISTENING AND
IT'S YOUR FAULT

Pam Marmon

no one's listening and it's your fault

GET YOUR MESSAGE HEARD DURING
ORGANIZATIONAL TRANSFORMATIONS

PAM HARALAKOVA MARMON

LIONCREST
PUBLISHING

NO ONE'S LISTENING AND IT'S YOUR FAULT
Get Your Message Heard During
Organizational Transformations

ISBN   978-1-5445-0711-8 *Hardcover*
   978-1-5445-0710-1 *Paperback*
   978-1-5445-0709-5 *Ebook*

To my darlings, John Henry, Gabriel, and Dominick—you set my world on fire.

To my beloved husband, Sam—you hold the flame.

Contents

Introduction

The Point of No Return

Imagine the moment when everyone in your company finds out your secret. You've spent months quietly developing an initiative that will transform your organization. You are getting ready for the grand unveiling, but now people have gotten wind that you are working on a change effort. Your diligent work behind closed doors has kindled rumors, and gossip has surfaced throughout your organization. You feel pressed against a wall. The inevitable announcement is looming, and you know it will disrupt the status quo.

The day of the announcement arrives. Your speech and presentation are polished. The stage is set and ready for the big reveal. The chairs are in perfect rows, one behind the other, empty and cold—for now.

You sift through your notes, palms sweating—yet you are confident because this is not your first time persuading a crowd. This time, however, the stakes are high. This is a message the company has been anticipating, and this message will change its future.

Will they rally behind the new vision? Will they still like you? What if they don't? Does it really matter?

You try to set these thoughts aside and go back to your notes. You reread the message. If only there was more time to rehearse it. You take in a deep breath and slowly let it out for a count of five, four, three, two, one.

People are filling the room one by one, with coffee in hand. You overhear chatter in the background. You smile, but on the inside, you are tense. The audience doesn't know you're nervous, and they never will.

You are an accomplished leader, vested in their success—and yours. You care deeply about your company's future. You care deeply about your people. Well... there are probably a few of them you would rather redirect. You shrug and focus back on your notes.

Now the auditorium is full and the time has arrived. The microphone is turned on. You hear your footsteps as you walk up to the podium. You shuffle your papers. The bright lights blind you for a moment. The audience's gaze is fixed on you. You clear your throat. *Ahem.*

There is absolute silence. You smile, and then you begin to speak. Your voice echoes through the room; the words flow out of your mouth and there is no snatching them back. This is the point of no return.

You hear a gasp. Someone claps. And then more silence. You hear some unexpected murmurs that surprise you.

And then it is over. Lights go out. The crowd shuffles out. You are once again alone, thinking about your message, the message you have cradled for months in preparation for this very day.

You take another deep breath. Now what?

Does this incident sound familiar? Could this be your story that unfolded on the pages you just read? Perhaps it takes you back to a moment in time when you had to deliver a message that would transform your organization. Was the outcome what you expected? Or was there silence?

Communicating company messages, especially messages of change, has its challenges. Do you think the majority of your employees could recite your organization's mission statement? A mission statement is the most critical communication artifact that defines the purpose and the path to achieve the organizational vision, and it has the power to motivate, inspire, engage, and propel employees into action. Communicating company messages, especially messages of change, can threaten the status quo. What can be expected of layered organizational messages like the one you delivered on that podium, messages that support the mission statement? Do they stand a chance of being recognized, let alone remembered?

Stuck and Frustrated

If you are a leader of an organization, it is likely that your grand vision and fast-paced approach to transformation can leave people frustrated and struggling to keep up. You commit to goals that require your teams to streamline processes and optimize the use of systems and technology. This shift demands that your people work differently.

Your messages sound relevant, but you question if anyone is listening. You drive for results, but you have created a whirlwind of change saturation. Your people are fatigued; they are exhausted, and some doubt you. Their silence explains their lack of action. They are on the verge of quitting, and you feel frustrated. The weight of pulling your team would be lighter if only people would hear your message and execute your vision!

The One Thing You Will Learn

This book is about one thing: **with the proper process, change is not hard.** I will teach you how to apply systematic change communication principles to lead transformations within your organization in order to achieve desired results and grow your impact.

The content of this book will help you understand:

1. Why others can't keep up with your pace
2. How to stage changes for fluid execution that delivers results
3. How you can approach the change process differently to unleash the powerful force of others
4. How to lead transformations through relevant and timely messages that promote lasting change

We will explore how the acronym LESS (listen, empower, speak, solve) will help you right-size and enhance your communication efforts as they relate to leading organizational change. By doing less of certain activities, you will benefit from more employee engagement, participation, support, and greater interest in transformation.

Benefits to Managed Change

According to research conducted by Prosci, a prominent change management research company, projects with excellent change management programs are six times more likely to achieve project objectives than those with poor change management programs.[1]

---

1   Prosci https://prosci.com.

Intentionally managing your organizational changes will enable you to accomplish the following:

- Increase the probability of success
- Manage employee resistance
- Minimize the impact of productivity loss
- Minimize turnover of valued employees
- Build change competency into the organization
- Deliver project results
- Enhance strong brand reputation

When you adopt the set of principles and implement the key change strategies outlined in the chapters that follow, you can help your organization grow and transform.

Your Role as a Leader of Change

When it comes to implementing change—and, specifically, communicating with your team—your role as a leader is to speak the language of your audience. The clarity of your message will eliminate confusion and inaction. The frequency of your message will establish cadence and a drumbeat to which others can sync.

As a leader of an organization, you are responsible for operating at a strategic level within your company and perhaps at times at a tactical level as well. When it comes to leading a transformation, you must manage the timing of changes to avoid change saturation. You have to communicate the purpose of the change frequently and through multiple channels. Additionally, you have to include others in decision-making to increase ownership and shared accountability. You must engage your team appropriately, seeking and acting on feedback. You have to acknowledge people's reactions and allow them to process the change. And, on top of all this, you must understand any resistance to the change and manage expectations, while reflecting on what is working and what needs to pivot.

Overwhelmed at the thought of this additional list of responsibilities to your already full schedule?

Instead of dreading these responsibilities, allow me to help you integrate them into your existing rhythm of business. But first, change starts with you: your awareness of the need for change, your understanding of human motivation, and your ability to cast a vision and alignment within your organization.

Change Is Not Hard

When I started to lead organizational change years ago, I bought into the mindset that change is hard. Because I believed change was difficult, I behaved like it was true. As a result, change *was* hard. However, as my experience and knowledge in the change management discipline grew, I began to challenge my previous assumption.

Change is often associated with pain and discomfort. We've been taught to avoid it, hide from it, and resist it. We've been conditioned to think that change is hard. Apart from the obvious change that interferes with our process of how things have been done, change implicates us on a deeper psychological and social level. Disruptive business change impacts our social interactions, our established authority and power, and our influence. Transformational change redefines the rules of the game. It shifts our perspective on what it takes to thrive and, in some cases, what it takes to survive.

Here are some ground rules that will transform how you think about change:

Every successful project requires change

While project management is about implementation,

change management is about adoption. You can't have one without the other; they are interdependent and integral to the success of any change effort.

Change is personal

People's first instinct is to understand the personal impact, or the "What's in it for me?" Once they have grappled with the answer, they can assist others on the change journey.

Change is emotional

Feelings are a more powerful change motivator than logic. As much as we'd like to believe we are rational human beings, our emotions undermine the logical part of our brain.

People commit to what they help shape and create, not what they are told

Everyone wants to be in control of his or her life. Instead of telling people what to do, help them craft their own hero journey with you.

Your audience is hungry for your message

People crave information. They want to consume it with delight and embrace the vision that's worthy of their time, their efforts, and their legacies.

People like progress; therefore, they desire change

Discover the deep desire of humanity to wrestle, adapt, and master the shifts of nature in search of comfort and control.

Everyone wants to change for the better, and everyone can

We as human beings are capable of adapting to change in search of growth, opportunities, and mastery of our environment.

If these statements make you feel uncomfortable, this book is for you. **With the proper process, change is not hard.**

A Different Outlook

In his book *Ricochet*, Nick Tasler addresses how our

mindset about change undermines our desired outcome and how "people who expect life to have challenges and hiccups not only cope better with stressful changes, they actually live longer."

What if we change our outlook about change? What if we actually think that change is everywhere and it serves us well to embrace it? What if we believe that everyone wants to change for the better, and now everyone can? What if we expect that our employees can change how they work and accomplish greater outcomes?

When you reset your mindset to embrace the redemptive power of change, you cease to plant seeds of doubt and begin to plant seeds of hope. When you believe that people want to change and that lasting change is achievable, you position your organization to receive and embrace a transformation. This is the most fulfilling and rewarding part of the transformative work we as leaders are called to pursue. As Juliet Funt says, "You, my dear leader, hold the pen that writes the story." You have a choice on how your story unfolds.

Consider this to be your story of applying a change communication strategy that works—but, most importantly, this is your story of being a trustworthy leader who has multiplied himself or herself within the organization, creating change through dynamic movement rather than a two-dimensional communication path.

The key to your success is hidden in the people you lead. Your leadership superpower is your people. Abuse it, and great harm will follow. Unleash it, and a magnitude of greatness will encompass you and refresh your soul. The choice is yours. What will your future be?

My Background

I know your pain because I've walked through it with you. I've helped you define your transformation. I've crafted your change strategy. I've talked with your people, I've listened to their concerns, I've sat in your meetings, I've drafted your messages, and I've watched you deliver them just like we planned. I've waited for the results to trickle. I've celebrated your successes and mourned your losses. And if I have to be honest with myself, I am like you: impatient, driven, and results oriented.

I have been leading change for as long as I can remember. Growing up in the Eastern European country of

Bulgaria has shaped my perspective on entrepreneurship and birthed a passion to change the world. Full of wonder, I envisioned a world with endless possibilities.

My personal and professional fascination with change management emerged early in my career, while working on an acquisition at a Fortune 50 high-tech client in Seattle. My work on this project propelled me to pursue further certification in change management, followed by years of practical industry application, obtaining an MBA, and teaching college-level courses on this topic.

I founded Marmon Consulting so I could continue to lead organizational transformations in the areas of emerging Future of Work initiatives, digital transformations, mergers and acquisitions, organizational restructures, new operating models, process improvements, and culture transformations. I wrote this book because I wholeheartedly believe that if we as leaders improve our ability to lead change, our world is a better place, our communities are more vibrant, our family lives thrive, and we are happier and more satisfied as individuals.

With the proper process, change is not hard. With

experience from Fortune 50s to startups, I have developed a broad understanding as I've led transformational initiatives in the aerospace, technology, insurance, healthcare, nonprofit, faith-based, financial, banking, corporate retail, and professional services industries, and more. This restorative work of change management has led me to conclude that I have the best job in the world, and I trust that you will find my passion and experience insightful as you transform your organization.

As a note, this book contains a collection of stories that represent the intricate journeys of the executive leaders I have been invited to guide through organizational transformations. To protect their confidentiality, I have changed the names and personality characteristics of my clients and have omitted the names of the companies they represent. Rest assured, the stories and examples are true as I recall them from my experience.

Enough about me. This book is about you.

In the chapters ahead, I will share how you can apply creative ways to engage your impacted stakeholders, amplify your message, and create a movement within your organization. The idea of leading change, regardless of how large or small, can trigger a myriad of emotions, ranging from excitement to frustration to doubt.

In the years I've helped leaders transform their organizations, I can assure you that you are not alone. While stepping into a transitional period with confidence is ideal, many leaders have doubts and uncertainty about the final outcome. It's OK not to have all the answers. No one is expecting you to know exactly what the future holds. A leader who is honest, trusted, and respected achieves more with people than one who appears to always be right.

It's understandable how a leader can fall victim to personal insecurities or to the stark reality of the current situation. Acknowledge the thoughts that hold you back so you can overcome them. Learn the strategies to confidently lead transformations with lasting results.

Allow me to join you on your journey. We will address the communication challenges first, and then explore the root causes, which rarely emerge unless we intentionally solve for them. Like an iceberg, the true obstacles to why you struggle to transform your organization lie deep below the surface.

Now, are you ready to tackle why your people are not listening to your messages during transformations? The most important transformation begins with you.

KEY TAKEAWAY

With the proper process, change is not hard.

PART I

Listen

———

CHAPTER 1

No One Is Listening and It's Your Fault

We have two ears and one mouth so that we can listen twice as much as we speak.

— EPICTETUS

"*It's your fault they don't know,*" I said. My words sat there. Silence filled the room as I waited for John to push back. After all, he was *my* mentor, and I had more to learn from him than vice versa. I knew his stakes were high and my response stunned him. It stunned me.

It was supposed to be a regular check-in at our usual place during our usual time. John was a senior leader with a distinguished record in serving our country and leading teams. He came from a military background and had accomplished much in his career. After exchanging greetings and commenting on our days, I asked John how his work was progressing. While I didn't know the specifics, I knew it was important work in a government contract company, which was impacting people in other parts of the organization, not to mention the tangible impact on our nation.

In attempting to communicate, John's team had sent email updates to their internal customers but received no response to the requests for action. To John's frustration, people were not reading the messages. Worse, they were disoriented about expectations and progress. John was about to miss a deadline and at his wit's end, just wishing people would read what he sent them and do their part.

Taking ownership of someone else's inactions is hard. It was difficult for John to see the role he played in this failure. The words rolled out of my mouth before I could catch them and tuck them away. *It's your fault they don't know.* People were not listening and it was John's fault.

The fact is that more than 70 percent of change efforts

fail, according to research conducted by Prosci. It happens so often that those of us in the change management discipline are aware of the potential loss a company is facing and work meticulously to address communication pitfalls and the underlying causes that derail projects and companies. In my experience, email in particular is the most ineffective way to communicate; yet, for many of us, it's our default communication channel.

If you lead an organization and people tell you they don't know what's going on, it is your fault.

Let me explain. As a leader, you have access to information that may never trickle down to your employees. It's likely that you see the big picture and can make sense of where the organization is headed. The majority of your people, on the other hand, are blind to the path toward the end goal. Your position grants you the privilege to see the future, and in return, it demands your ability to inform others of what's ahead.

Effective leaders understand that by communicating important information multiple times, people can grasp how that information will impact them. To ensure that the messages reach the desired final destination, you have to deploy multiple communication channels throughout your organization.

There are a plethora of challenges a company can face when implementing change. For a growing number of organizations, remote work has led to infrequent physical paths crossing. Maybe you feel the pressure of lofty objectives and it's hard to keep projects moving forward? Or you need to expand your team to accomplish the work? If not addressed, it's likely these challenges will create a disconnect within your team and birth a considerable discomfort for decision-making that delays your work.

If your vision is to transform your organization, your team, or even yourself, it's likely you, like John, have experienced frustration and questioned others who were incapable of keeping up. You may have committed to deadlines just to find yourself stretching them out in hopes that more time will get your team on board. Perhaps your organization is change saturated. Or the opposite—perhaps it rarely undergoes significant change and people don't know how to behave during a transformation. Maybe your people are fatigued, exhausted, or on the brink of quitting? Maybe you need to hire new team members, or reframe the vision of the organization?

The reality is that your career success depends on your ability to lead change, and if you fail to master that skill, it will jeopardize your future.

There are no simple solutions to resolve these challenges. A healthy, high-functioning organization operates effectively across its departments and understands how a shift in strategy will impact everyone. It is a rare company that is able to exceptionally master its operations, especially as an organization matures and grows. The complexity of work can cloud our ability to synchronize our communications.

People are not listening, and unless you captivate their minds and their hearts, you will miss the opportunity to engage them in meaningful ways.

Why People May Not Be Listening

Change is a process. When we manage it, we enable employees to adapt faster by aligning stakeholders through shared vision, value proposition, impact, and expectations. The benefits to the business include faster speed to market, increased efficiency, stronger brand, and more empowered employees. To pass the test for effective transformation, consider these must-haves:

- There must be a compelling reason for both employees and the organization to change.
- There must be urgency.
- There must be a strong leader to sponsor the change.
- There must be a clear vision.
- There must be a plan to execute the change.
- There must be a network of influencers championing the work.
- There must be clear communications with the "What's in it for me?"

Balance is essential so that your message does not overpower your people, or underwhelm them to the point of disinterest. The interwoven ecosystem that leads to success is inclusive of your organization's culture, talent, capabilities, agility, industry, global economy, and collective leadership skills.

But What If Your Messages Are Relevant and *Still* No One Is Listening?

Have you heard the Bible story of the parable of the sower? This parable describes a hardworking farmer who sows seeds in the land. Some seeds fall on fertile soil, while others fall in thorny land on the side of the road. Like the sower, you may have diligently been communicating relevant messages through multiple channels, and yet struggle to get engagement. Your answer may be tangled in a combination of thorny reasons.

It's Not the Right Message

You may be communicating a complicated message that is disconnected from the overall messages that flow throughout the organization. Your message may be too vague or too detailed. People are confused by what you ask of them, and they ignore the message—or worse, they ignore you.

It's Not the Right Timing

This culprit has many victims. Timing can be broken into two categories: timing of messages and organizational timing.

Timing of Messages

In his book *When*, Daniel Pink addresses the importance of the timing of daily activities. His research points out that there is an enormous impact on the desired outcomes based on when you perform certain tasks. Pink categorizes the day in three cycles: peak periods are best for analytical and focused work; trough periods are best for administrative work; and recovery periods are best for creative work. Be intentional about the timing of your messages so that your end receivers are in their prime state to hear them. I advise all my clients to avoid sending important organizational messages at the end of the week on Friday or near holiday periods. It is likely those messages would not be heard appropriately or embraced as intended.

Organizational Timing

If there are more significant changes taking place in your organization, your message will likely get lost. The sequence of large transformational messages within your organization is important to your end receivers. If there are messages about layoffs, your project messages will likely be secondary, at best, to the critical information circulating within your organization. Be aware and mindful of your organization's ecosystem so you can space important messages accordingly.

You Are Not the Right Sender

Now this feels personal. Sometimes it is, but not always. According to the extensive research done by Prosci, employees expect to hear organizational vision messages from the executive leaders, while they expect messages about changes to their day-to-day work to come from their direct manager. This may be a question of adequate position and authority, or a question of trust and respect. Regardless, who sends the message is as important as the message itself.

Your Organizational Culture Is Dysfunctional

You may have heard the expression, "Culture eats strategy for breakfast." This one may or may not be entirely in your control. People in your organization may have lost trust in the executive leaders and, as a result, disengaged from the work. Sick organizations have many symptoms of brokenness. Inefficient communication is just one among a slew of possible areas that need urgent attention.

Your Message Is Not Aligned

The story you are telling doesn't make sense in the context of the organizational environment. It's fragmented, out of place, and you've failed to make the connections between urgency for action and where the organization is going.

You Haven't Told People What to Do

Some communications are well crafted, but miss an important component—they don't outline step by step exactly what people need to do. If there is no specific action, your message won't be heard and implemented. Due to the large volume of daily information consumed, people are scanning your messages for what's expected of them. If they can't quickly identify that content, they will likely preserve brainpower for more pressing activities that require their action.

If your transformation messages are not being heard, somewhere along the journey, you missed a step, jumped too far, turned too fast, and went off course.

Now what?

Leading Successful Transformations: How to Get People to Listen

If you want to lead successful transformations, think of

your message as a piece of a puzzle. Without context to see how it fits, people won't know its purpose or what to do with it.

Leading change is complex, and much can get in the way. I know this because I've seen how the wrong timing, the unprepared leader, the change-saturated organization, the resistant employee, the lack of change champions, the wrong project, or [fill in your reason here] have crumbled organizations and left good leaders feeling inadequate. Good employees have left good companies, and good companies have lost good revenue and good results. Perhaps the most disheartening part is that when good work goes unfinished, good people suffer. My heart aches when the world loses out on the benefits of your good efforts.

How to Make the Most of This Book

Over the years, I've developed an approach with my clients. I now want to teach you this methodical and practical approach to planning and executing change. Each chapter of this book is designed to walk you through a systematic process to get your message heard within your organization.

1. Read each chapter as it relates to the specific change communication topic.
2. Download the Change Communication Strategy template found on marmonconsulting.com/no_ ones_listening.
3. Complete the action items listed at the end of each chapter.

Each chapter will address a different component of the change communication strategy, which is a part of the overall change management plan. The steps are somewhat sequential, and I advise you to read the chapters in order. This chapter gave you a taste of why your messages may not be landing well within your organization. In the pages ahead, you'll assess whether your efforts are overwhelming your team and how to hear what people don't want to tell you. Once you have an understanding of your current challenges, you will discover and apply techniques to get your message multiplied and cascaded throughout your organization.

Some of this will come to you intuitively, while certain parts will feel frustrating because they require you to engage others and take more time than you can dedicate. While communication is a significant component of leading change, it's just that: a component.

It is central to execution, but so is the ability to drive desired behaviors, align incentives, and shift current mindsets to establish new organizational values. There's an art and science to that part, and yes, I will help you think through that as well.

Conclusion

On one level, this book is about effectively leading organizational change through relevant communications. I will teach you how to do that part, and then I will ask you to come along with me *beyond* that point. Transform your organization by erasing the marks of past fears and step into a new leadership outlook where your people *want* to change your organization with you. They see themselves as part of a solution beyond their work, and you will lead them to a vision larger than your department, bigger than your division, and beyond your company's mission. Lead them to the greater good of humankind. Lead them to impact.

Now back to the basics: change communications.

People may not be listening because your message is only a piece of the puzzle. Give it context and help people see how and why it fits in your organization.

Consider the change you are leading and complete these action items:

DOWNLOAD PDF:

MarmonConsulting.com/No_Ones_Listening

- ☐ Go to marmonconsulting.com/no_ones_listening and download the Change Communication Strategy template.
- ☐ Complete the Vision section of the template.
- ☐ Write a cohesive message that integrates into the context of the organizational vision.

☐ Communicate the "why" message to invite people along the journey.

CHAPTER 2

You're Doing Too Much

The barrier to change is not too little caring; it is too much complexity. To turn caring into action, we need to see a problem, see a solution, and see the impact. But complexity blocks all three steps.

—BILL GATES

Change saturation is your enemy.

I had a client, Karen, who was an adventure traveler to exotic locations. Karen was a brilliant, driven leader who worked at a nonprofit company with an impeccable track record for changing the world. The culture was one of excellence, intelligence, progressive thought leadership, and exceptional accomplishments. Because the stakes were high and the organization demanded results, this was one of my most intense engagements to date. I was early in my change management career, and I did everything by the book. Literally, I walked around with a thick, overly highlighted change manual in hand and followed the process that promised results. I must admit, there was a vast chasm between what the work demanded and my skills at that time.

Karen's team was responsible for reforming the core-operating model of the organization. This was no small task, since it would have ripple effects across the organization's humanitarian efforts in the world. Months of planning, gathering assessments, conducting workshops, and strategizing led to the launch of the multiyear initiative. The team was buzzing with excitement because the work was impactful, and we were determined to make a difference.

Our comprehensive change plans included stakeholder engagement activities and voice of the customer interviews, as well as how our communications would unfold. We had identified formal and informal channels, various messages during the milestones, and key senders who were change influencers. Some messages were polished, while others were intentionally designed to feel organic, nimble, and efficient, such as handwritten notes on whiteboards in common spaces throughout the office buildings. After all, we were driving for speed and wanted our communications to portray the subtle, desired behaviors. We wanted staged messages to become conversations that would carry on in the hallways beyond the meetings.

We launched our communication campaign and waited with anticipation, but there was more noisy chatter than insightful progress. Our messages went into the void as we watched the client's employees get buried beneath countless emails and back-to-back meetings. Keeping the pace became an impossible endeavor. The underlying rhythm of operation swept us away into what felt like an endless circular motion.

So why did we stumble? While our content was on target, we failed to integrate our messages within the larger story that was being told across the organization. As it turned out, this particularly ambitious client had multiple priorities across various departments. Imagine the confusion we collectively created when people received multiple messages from multiple leaders on multiple projects. The organization was change saturated, and we missed the opportunity to effectively align and integrate our efforts with those of our peers. Our messages felt muted.

Change Saturation: How to Fight It

Have you ever experienced a season in your personal and professional life when it felt as if everything around you was changing? Most of us have felt that way and can relate to a similar experience when relocating to a new city, starting a new job, settling into a new home, or establishing yourself in a new community. It takes a significant amount of energy to make progress on multiple fronts.

This is known as change saturation. When we become change saturated, it's normal to feel like giving up or intentionally focusing your efforts only on your top priorities. You may have learned to cope with the stress by exercising, managing your thoughts to focus on the present rather than the unknown future, talking to friends and family, asking for help, or processing your emotions. You may pray or meditate, practice deep breathing, or listen to soothing music to relax your body and mind. At work, you may unknowingly ignore the bustle of busyness and listen only for the relevant messages to help you cope and survive. These are normal responses when we face change saturation.

An abundance of change and the exhaustion that comes with it is common in most of the organizations I work with. As leaders, we are responsible for mindfully structuring the upcoming transformations and adjusting our expectations for how our people will experience the constant shifts. We must pay attention to the change curve.

Decrease the Dip

Perhaps you are familiar with the change curve, which is an adaptation of Elisabeth Kübler-Ross' stages of grief curve. At the moment a change is introduced, most people have no prior awareness of it. The immediate reaction after the news becomes public is to think about how the change will personally impact them, regardless of whether the change is positive or negative. Soon after, they dip into what is often described as "the valley of despair," where productivity is at its lowest. This stage of coping with change requires people to dig deep to find their own motivations and the amount of effort they are willing to invest to move forward with the transition. They may experience grief, but eventually emerge with hope, which takes them to engagement and, ultimately, ownership of the change. The path may look different for those who resist the change. They may find themselves parting ways with the organization and beginning a new journey with another company. However, it's likely that another change will emerge, it will throw them off equilibrium, and the cycle begins again. To prevent being a victim of change, it's important to learn how to live with change and adapt. In chapter 7, we'll talk a bit about being the hero of your story and empowering employees to feel the same way. Throughout our careers, we embrace change because we have to adapt to our new environment, and we manage change, so we don't become obsolete and irrelevant.

While they're more complex at an organizational level than at a personal level, the emotions associated with change stay consistent. We become anxious, unfocused, scattered, and unproductive. That triggers a set of unfortunate consequences. Key employees leave, engagement plummets, customers complain, and profits suffer.

But there is a better way!

Leading change is about speaking to people's feelings so that you can transform their behavior. In the case of my ambitious client, Karen, we mitigated the risk by assembling a team of project leaders from the various large initiatives across the organization. We decided that the best way to understand what the organization was experiencing was to map out the projects in Excel, overlaying them on top of each other against the calendar timeline and a list of stakeholder groups. This allowed us to see when the organization would experience a high amount of change, and when there were restful seasons of organizational change. Then we began to coordinate.

By not considering other departmental changes when we first rolled out the initiative, we had ignored the end receiver. The overall company story wasn't cohesive to the end receiver, and so they tuned out instead of tuning in. This time, we corrected that mistake. We focused as much as possible on improving the stakeholders' experience. By coordinating, we were able to tell a cohesive story that incorporated initiatives across the organization, and we collectively benefitted from the successful outcomes.

Alignment and Growth

Research indicates that "companies with aligned

marketing and sales teams experience an average of 20 percent growth in annual revenue."[2] As a leader of your company, your daily pursuit of alignment prevents potential mishaps between departments. Each department must understand its own function and the function of other departments, as well as their dependencies, which support the life of the organization. Once you know what is important to other leaders, create the space and time to help them achieve success. The desire to help other leaders succeed can be reciprocated back to you through greater collaboration and goodwill among employees.

Types of Organizational Alignment

There are two types of organizational alignment that are necessary for change to thrive: (1) alignment across departments and (2) alignment across initiatives. Without proper alignment, teams operate in silos and with limited visibility into the operating priorities within the organization. Communication is the key to unlock the required conversations and collaboration.

---

2   Jeff Boss, "A Simple Flow for Thinking About Organizational Alignment," *Forbes*, January 21, 2018 https://www.forbes.com/sites/jeffboss/2018/01/21/a-simple-flow-to-think-about-organizational-alignment/#5c87a77c3df4.

Alignment across Departments

We changed Karen's story to a successful case by focusing on change alignment across departments. Everyone wins when leaders work together. You must learn what your peers in the organization are doing and how you can support them in achieving their objectives. Your genuine interest in the work of others has multiple benefits. It is foundational for effective teamwork, it fosters collaboration across departments, it primes the organization for executive championing of key initiatives, and it establishes trust and alignment.

You can combat change saturation by focusing on change alignment across departments to create a cohesive company story. This alignment is crucial. It is not only beneficial for you and your career, but it is also important for the experience of your people, who have limited exposure to initiatives outside their department. Satisfy their hunger by communicating how other departments are also moving the organization forward in support of the overall vision, so that they can envision the collective effort of their colleagues.

Alignment across Initiatives

Here's another example of creating a cohesive story.

A client of mine, Jeff, who was a culinary enthusiast, was implementing an Agile framework from a technology standpoint, as well as from a cultural mindset shift. The Agile iterative approach organizes teams to innovate within shorter cycles, while providing early feedback and incremental delivery. This transformation required the IT department to set aside its traditional project management Waterfall methods, which apply a sequential process and embrace a new way of working with its business partners. For the rest of the organization, applying Agile principles meant looking for improvements, continuously evaluating processes, and being nimble and quick to adapt to changes in the environment.

Jeff's story is an example of alignment across departments and initiatives. While this effort supported the strategic direction of the organization, applying it in the company's day-to-day operations required Jeff's team to craft intentional messages to help departments align and embrace a new way of working together. To layer the messages in addition to other important initiatives risked our chances of being heard.

As a consultant, I recommended we layer our messages and integrate our content in the context of an existing, highly visible initiative. In their case, this initiative was a Career Architecture project that was being rolled out to the entire organization. You may be wondering: what does Agile and Career Architecture have in common? In the case of this particular client, they were both part of the organization's strategic plan, which provided the natural intersection for us to leverage a blended message.

Since the Career Architecture work was several months ahead of the Agile project, it gave us the opportunity to leverage already existing messages and embed them into ours. The goal was for impacted stakeholders to hear about the Agile effort linked with the Career Architecture undertones. We wanted to tell a narrative that showed people how they would benefit from embracing an Agile mindset. The Career Architecture work laid the foundation for us to build a story that took people a step beyond having a career path. A satisfying career through continuous improvement was the mindset for both the individual and the organization.

Aligning Change with Your Company's Vision

The key to success is for your change effort to align with the overall organizational strategy. If your organization lacks a compelling vision and comprehensive strategic plan, all efforts become secondary in importance and priority. Without a vision, an organization aimlessly churns work and portrays an illusion of progress.

Why We Don't Do Organizational Alignment Well

Achieving organizational alignment can be a herculean task. Once the organizational vision is established, the executive leaders need to communicate it across the organization. Often, those important messages don't make it through the appropriate channels, and people miss out on receiving a comprehensive set of directions.

What if the organizational vision is commonly shared? The next challenge is that it may be difficult to coordinate everyone's top priorities. You may have heard the saying, "If everything is important, nothing is." Large initiatives have many moving parts and frequent changes of direction, which can lead to confusion and a standstill. Leaders need to skillfully navigate office politics, while their teams are frantically producing and maintaining a state of busyness.

How to Do Organizational Alignment Well

There are no shortcuts to creating strategic alignment. It begins with a vision that rallies people for a greater purpose. It is founded on trust among the executive leaders, camaraderie across department managers, accessible information, timely and accurate data, visible progress, and celebrated accomplishments. This is an enormous undertaking for any organization. This stuff is important. The risk associated with lazy leadership crumbles organizations and leaves unfulfilled missions in the world. We must acknowledge the hard work that is required and get to work, because if we don't, we will be solving the same problems year after year. **Strategic alignment is at the core of leading successful organizational change.**

Back to my client Jeff. We had aligned change across initiatives (Agile and Career Architecture) to create a cohesive company story, but the program was stuck. We hosted well-designed workshops, the team was engaged and excited for the future, but when it came time to do the work, little progress was made week after week. Why?

It was time for a difficult conversation.

"Why are we not moving forward?" I asked. The initial response was that we lacked the skills. I kept probing for the real reason why the work had stalled. Several layers deep, we discovered the origin of the struggle—uncertainty and confusion around the alignment and how the work supports the organization's vision. This uncertainty escalated as the most important task to resolve. Once clarity was established, the change effort was reinforced.

Conclusion

While the purpose of this book is to help you effectively communicate during organizational transformations, we have to set the stage so that your efforts are well-positioned and received by impacted stakeholders. Lack of proper strategy alignment confuses people. Not only do you need to have a vision for your initiative, but your initiative also needs to fit within the overall strategy of your organization. **Without organizational alignment, your messages won't stick.** There may be curiosity at first, but the interest will fade if people lack understanding about how the work impacts them and moves the organization forward.

Consider the change you are leading and complete these action items:

☐ Go to marmonconsulting.com/no_ones_listening and download the Change Communication Strategy template.

☐ Learn or inquire what other leaders in the organization are doing and how you can support them in achieving success.

☐ Align your work in the context of the organization for a cohesive narrative that people in the organization understand.

☐ Complete the Alignment section in the template.

CHAPTER 3

You Don't Know It All

The pessimist complains about the wind; the optimist expects it to change; the realist adjusts the sails.

—WILLIAM ARTHUR WARD

For days, I stared intently at my screen, searching for visual clues to our problem. I was working with a client, Rebecca, who was tasked with rolling out a remote work program in her organization. Rebecca was a marathon runner who was up for the challenge. The benefits of the remote work program seemed clear; after all, this was the future of work. What was unclear was the resistance that bubbled up from the interviews with managers.

Everyone had smiled and told us how beneficial it would be to allow employees to work remotely. After all, that was the direction of the chief HR officer, and it aligned well with the strategic priorities of the organization. Technology today allows us to seamlessly work virtually from anywhere in the world. Rolling this program out across the organization was a step into the future.

Virtual work is not a new concept, and it isn't revolutionary by any means. If you hire the right people and give them the tools to do their job, they will deliver, right? The implementation in this organization was slightly more challenging—the directive was that all qualifying employees could now work remotely. It was no longer a privilege; it was how work was to be done. This was a culture shift!

However, it wasn't working. Some people were not warming up to the idea, and the interviews were telling us so.

You Don't Know It All: The Readiness Assessment

How often do you set time aside to conduct interviews

before you launch into a transformational initiative? In my practice, this is a mandatory activity for every large transformation. With the excitement of the recently announced project, many leaders want to dive in and get to work. It is convenient to skip the interviews and plunge straight into the design phase of the project. Resist the temptation if you want to apply the right change management approach and achieve your desired results.

In every business change initiative, there is potential resistance that is "unknown." It's like putting a puzzle together without having the picture to show you how the pieces fit together. But just like a puzzle, there are key pieces that give clues and signals that steer you in the right direction. There are foundational principles that stand out and provide stability and direction. If unnoticed, the unknown can sabotage the transformational efforts. Readiness Assessments help you clarify what you don't know.

The key to creating a successful customized change management approach is hidden in the results of the Readiness Assessment. Failure to extract data from the impacted stakeholders will significantly increase the probability of missed expectations.

While I refer to the interviews as Readiness Assessments, in the field of change management, they are also known as Stakeholder Assessments and Impact Assessments. Over the years, I've collected a set of standard questions, and I customize a few more to ensure that I get the exact data that I want specific to each project. It is no secret that I thoroughly enjoy conducting the interviews. With experience, I've learned that if I conduct the interviews well, it's not the questions that I ask that will give me the data I want, but the question after the question after the question where rich data resides. My role is to establish trust with the interviewee, keep confidentiality, and solve for the unknown, which is the answer to making the change stick.

Why We Neglect to Conduct Organizational Assessments

Conducting organizational assessments requires time and resources. Most leaders hastily move past the assessments because they believe to already have a good grasp on their organization, or they are afraid to see what their people truly think about them and the work that's ahead. We tend to be skeptical of the unknown, and it is no surprise that we omit the practice of an in-depth assessment. It can be perceived as an activity that slows down the work, incurs incremental resources, and highlights flaws that are unmanageable.

Ambitious leaders want to move ahead, but I ask you to move ahead armed with data, grounded perspective, and a well-rounded change management approach to address and overcome the obstacles you will face.

Conducting Readiness Assessments

The purpose of a Readiness Assessment is to provide you with information to formulate the change management efforts. As a leader, your role is to ensure that participants feel empowered to share information that will remain confidential and anonymous. Working with a neutral party or consultant ensures that you will get raw, pure feedback that will help you make decisions regarding implementation.

There are several benefits to conducting a Readiness Assessment. In addition to helping you define the change management plan, it provides you with an opportunity for feedback and engagement.

- **Share information:** A well-crafted Readiness Assessment will draw out insights and arm stakeholders with key messages that will strengthen your informal communication channels.

- **Gather input:** By selecting the most fitting questions, you obtain valuable insights and a baseline to benchmark your starting point as it relates to your people.

- **Generate ideas:** If you want to test concepts and find alternative solutions, you can include open-ended questions that draw out creative ideas.

- **Make decisions:** Perhaps the most significant benefit of a Readiness Assessment is that it provides you with data to make decisions so that people believe their ideas matter and their leadership understands what is at stake.

The key factor to a successfully executed Readiness Assessment is a seasoned interviewer, who knows when to sit in the awkwardness of the silence, when to ask a probing question, and when to simply listen because it's the right thing to do. After years of conducting interviews, I'm often told how therapeutic the experience was for the interviewees because someone cared to listen to their concerns. It is a privilege to earn people's trust, and I don't take it lightly when others disclose their worries, anger, and raw emotions. Empathy is the path to people's hearts.

What Questions to Ask

Selecting the appropriate questions to ask during the interviews is critical to get the desired results. There are several categories I reference, depending on the scope of the transformation and the information that I have obtained prior to the interviews. The more background I have on the organization and the leaders, the more specific questions I select to ask.

It's important to make the most of the time with the interviewees so I can obtain accurate data and avoid the need for additional inquiries. The Readiness Assessment is designed to propel the adoption of the desired outcomes. I keep the focus on moving the organization forward while learning what has and has not worked in the past, and asking only questions that provide leaders with actionable data.

Since most interviews last thirty minutes, I select six to eight questions from my priority categories, which include the following:

- Past changes
- Culture
- Leadership capability
- Case for change

- Stakeholder impact
- Awareness for the need to change
- Desire to change
- Motivation
- Behaviors
- Communication
- Training
- Resistance management
- Influencers
- Accountability

Each category has a set of specific questions, including numerical, ranking, rating, multiple-choice, and open-ended questions. Customizing the questions to fit the organizational change is required in order to obtain specific insights to enable the adoption of the change. For specific sample questions or to find help as you craft and conduct your Readiness Assessment, check out our blog at marmonconsulting.com.

Who Needs to Participate?

Selecting the appropriate participants provides you with targeted data for the impacted stakeholders. Consider selecting a blend of influencers from various impacted groups. It's helpful to have the perspective of executives and managers, as well as front-line employees. I cap most of my interviews at twenty participants because I rarely get net new insights by including more people. Some organizational cultures are highly inclusive and feel obligated to involve more participants than necessary. At a minimum, include a representative from each impacted area. Anything beyond the necessary becomes a distraction and can dilute or skew the data.

Once the Readiness Assessments have been completed, the interviewer will provide a findings report along with recommendations and next steps. As a leader of this change, it is critical to acknowledge the feedback your team provides, regardless of whether you decide to implement the recommendations. People want to be heard, and this is the time for you to listen.

What If You Don't Agree?

"I'd like to change the Readiness Assessment," said the executive sponsor, Lucy.

I had made a rookie mistake, and I knew it. After multiple attempts on my part to privately share the results of the Readiness Assessment with Lucy, scheduling and other priorities got in the way. Lucy was a mother of twin teenage boys who traveled to play competitive soccer. Needless to say, Lucy was gracefully balancing work-life responsibilities. Against my better judgment, Lucy received the Readiness Assessment report along with the people on the project team. Unfortunately, the meeting was much larger than necessary. We had over forty people on the call, most of whom rarely ever spoke. I shared the report, and silence filled the room as Lucy made her request. She wanted to change the report because it surfaced an organizational challenge that was not favorable. But there we were in front of her team who provided that data, and hiding it would jeopardize the validity of their input.

Beware. It's likely that the Readiness Assessment will include information that you expected to see, and some information that may surprise you. If there is no constructive data, someone is not doing you a favor and is trying to please you. Our natural inclination is to want to augment the report in our favor, but I urge you to pause and observe the ideas and reactions of your team. Take time to be still and listen. You may be delighted to find out something you did not know. It's likely the most valuable insight you will get from your team. Consider it their gift to you.

Why You Need a Consultant

While my objective is not to convince you to hire a change management consultant, I strongly recommend you do so for this activity. A consultant provides a neutral perspective and can remain objective when tension surfaces. Everything I teach in this book can be done in-house *only if* you have the right skills and have allocated adequate resources to be successful. Many clients presume they can tackle change management in-house, but fail to allocate incremental time so the assigned person can properly navigate the change.

One benefit of working with a consultant is that it provides a neutral party who can represent both the leadership team and the impacted stakeholders. Learning how to complete templates and follow a prescribed process can be taught. It is more difficult to teach the ability to navigate cultural challenges and political agendas so that the success of the work is not compromised. The most seasoned consultants are able to quickly integrate within your organizational culture and navigate uncharted paths by establishing trusting relationships.

To help you avoid a catastrophic mistake, I want to warn you that if the change plans are not customized to your organization and your specific initiative, the initiative will be at risk. While utilizing a less-experienced person may be more affordable, it will take longer and can be more costly due to mistakes made along the way. Working with a more senior person will be more expensive, but you may be able to dodge pitfalls and lead more effectively.

From Readiness Assessments to Results

Let's go back to Rebecca, who was implementing a remote work program in her organization. Based on our initial interviews and Readiness Assessments, we found that the resistance was coming from managers, who perceived remote working as a way of losing control over the performance of their teams. Managers feared their own skills gap to manage remote workers and were hesitant to extend trust to their employees to get work done outside the corporate office space.

Now that we understood the problem, we could fix it. To combat their concerns, the majority of change management efforts targeted and enabled managers to thrive in the new way of leading virtual teams (we will explore this in greater detail in chapter 5). We began collecting data at the completion of each wave and were pleasantly surprised to discover that their worries did not come to fruition. Managers ranked themselves the highest on their own ability to manage their remote teams and expressed great satisfaction around the benefits of the program. By taking the time to interview key stakeholders before implementation and measuring the critical points of resistance, we overcame potential tension and ensured the success of the work.

Conclusion

By conducting a Readiness Assessment, you will benefit from key insights that enable you to proactively mitigate people-related risks and address anticipated resistance. Inviting your people to have a voice in the process anchors their commitment and benefits the execution of the change by increasing adoption in the long run. While this activity can consume several weeks to complete, the buy-in from your team is worthy of the investment.

KEY TAKEAWAY

There is power in the voice of many. If people believe their ideas are heard, their actions will follow.

Consider the change you are leading and complete these action items:

- ☐ Go to marmonconsulting.com/no_ones_listening and download the Change Communication Strategy template.
- ☐ Conduct a Readiness Assessment.
- ☐ Ask people for insights to help you determine how to lead your change initiative.
- ☐ Genuinely listen to and acknowledge the feedback you receive.
- ☐ Complete the Feedback section in the template.

PART 2

Empower

CHAPTER 4

———

Share the Podium

Without trust we don't truly collaborate; we merely coordinate or, at best, cooperate. It is trust that transforms a group of people into a team.

—STEPHEN COVEY

It was a "David and Goliath" Old Testament kind of interaction, but this time it wasn't David who held the victory. This time it was Goliath who swung the sling.

Acquisitions are hard and messy, especially when they impact global organizations with different cultures. Stacy was a client of mine with an extensive career in product management and also a scratch golfer. She worked for a Fortune 50 technology client that made a strategic decision to acquire another technology company and leverage its product to enhance its existing portfolio. This was an intentional acquisition that, over time, proved to be profitable, but there were bumps in the road that were not limited to the technology side.

According to the *Harvard Business Review* article "So Many M&A Deals Fail Because Companies Overlook This Simple Strategy,"[3] the predominant reason for failed mergers and acquisitions was due to lack of synergy. The authors analyzed the successful acquisition between Procter & Gamble and Gillette: "While some cost synergies were realized, the real payoff came because each company independently recognized that it had the permission to expand what it was offering to its core customers and that the capabilities to deliver on this potential resided in the other company."

They contrast this example with eBay's acquisition of Skype, a merger and acquisition that did not benefit from the intended synergy. While eBay executives expected customers to welcome the ability to use video chat to complete online auctions, the customers did

---

3   Alan Lewis and Dan McKone, "So Many M&A Deals Fail Because Companies Overlook This Simple Strategy," *Harvard Business Review*, May 10, 2016 https://hbr. org/2016/05/so-many-ma-deals-fail-because-companies-overlook-this-simple-strategy.

not embrace that feature, which resulted in a lack of synergy between the two companies.

While financial estimates take the lead, cultural synergies determine if the companies are destined to integrate. By design, some mergers and acquisitions are not intended for success, as the companies do not integrate well. But for those companies that become interdependent on each other, underestimating the importance of the team dynamics can be fatal to the organization.

Culture assimilation has its own set of challenges. To effectively integrate the two organizations, Stacy, at my Fortune 50 technology client, relied on the "insiders." Those were the influencers who were ingrained into the soon-to-be acquired organization, and they had foresight regarding the direction of the work. Essentially, they were insiders in both organizations, and they possessed the ability to morph and represent their peers and leadership.

In our attempt to assimilate the people, we had regular meetings to learn about the "water cooler" conversations, what people were concerned about, and if there was chatter about potential talent loss. We took the pulse of the organization and adjusted the communications to match the needs. This deeply ingrained attention to the impacted people paved the way for a successful integration.

Why We Fail to Invite Others

One of the best ways to amplify your message is to leverage key influencers in your organization. Most leaders simply miss the opportunity to empower others because they are not intentionally pursuing this goal. Timelines, budgets, KPIs, and the expectations of running a business can crowd out "inclusion." Yet it is inclusion that will unlock the key to engagement, which ultimately leads to ownership and accountability.

Unlock the Executive Level

When we leverage key influencers in organizations, we magnify our message, especially when the influencers are at the executive level. At the rudimentary level, every person wants to know "What's in it for me?'" For a leader, we can expand that to include "What's in it for me and my team?" To engage another executive leader, you need to tell a compelling story that connects to how your work will help them accomplish their strategic goals. I have often found that success hides in the intersection of two unique disciplines. As a leader, the amount of time and effort you dedicate to strengthening your relationships with executive leaders is critical to the success of your work. When multiple leaders move the organization together in the same direction, people follow. **A leader's ability to persuade executives to champion the work will determine the depth of reach and impact within the organization.**

Unlock the Manager Level

According to research on the *Best Practices in Change Management* conducted by Prosci, people want to receive communications about company strategy from the executive leaders, and they want to receive communications about changes to their day-to-day job from their direct manager. Leaders in managerial positions expect to be actively engaged with their teams. They are hungry for relevant information they can share to empower people within the organization. They face the challenge of opposing priorities from both their leaders and their team members.

Communicating with managers is one of the most

overlooked and underutilized areas with the greatest opportunity for impact.

Remember Rebecca, from chapter 3? Rebecca was an HR leader for one of my insurance clients. The organization was implementing a remote work program for all of its employees in order to attract and retain skilled talent. The company was located in multiple states, and various teams were already embracing remote work. After conducting a change Readiness Assessment, I discovered that the greatest resistance came from managers who were unsure how to do performance management since they could no longer observe their employees. The employees were concerned about the loss of social interactions and the potential lack of career progression. Knowing this valuable information, I helped Rebecca and her team to create a change management strategy that prioritized the support of the managers. This approach ensured that we addressed employee concerns through the communications we provided to the managers. We empowered the managers with information and trusted them to lead their teams through the transitional period, to great success.

Unlock the Peer-to-Peer Level

Remember your middle-school years, when overcoming peer pressure was the key to survival? Peer pressure is powerful, effective (for better or worse), and it sticks. It's surprising how much we can learn and apply from the past to influence people in the workplace. Perhaps a more fitting term for it in the workplace is "peer approval." This is the sweeping momentum that takes place when an increasing volume of supporters begin to emerge. Peer approval works, but be careful! If used incorrectly or with the wrong motive, it will backfire. Proceed with caution.

The reason peer approval works is because people have a natural desire for acceptance and approval. Most of us want to be wanted, we seek to belong, we adapt so that we can be like others, and we fear failure and rejection. Flying solo takes a lot of effort. If we blend into the organizational culture, we can get farther.

Deploy Change Champions

Let's go back to Stacy's story of the insiders, with which we opened this chapter. We empowered people through the use of change champions. This is a highly impactful tactic that allows individuals within your organization to benefit from social approval and the momentum gained through peer-to-peer influence. Change champions demonstrate commitment to the change initiative, increase the speed of adoption, personalize communications, and provide valuable feedback from their peers.

Who Are Your Change Champions?

When identifying change champions, consider individuals who are well respected and trusted in the organization. The ideal change champion will have influence, with or without a lucrative, prestigious job title. The person will be sought out for insights, direction, and information. This is also a great opportunity to include high-potential individuals in your organization in need of development opportunities. The selection process is important and needs to be inclusive of the impacted stakeholder groups. It is not necessary for change champions to agree with the change you are leading. In most cases, it is beneficial to also include individuals who oppose the work, so you can gain perspective into their resistance. Individuals who resist the change could offer you the most valuable information to help others in your organization overcome challenges and adapt to the new way of work.

What Is the Role of Change Champions?

Have you ever wanted to hear an interesting detail from an insider? Perhaps something leaders wouldn't stumble upon on their own or successfully encourage people to disclose in a company-wide survey? Change champions provide those kinds of insights. Simply stated, the role of a change champion is threefold:

1. Provide feedback from within the organization.
2. Share information within their sphere of influence.
3. Advocate on behalf of the project by demonstrating new behaviors and mindset shifts.

Helping change agents understand what is expected of them will clarify how you plan to engage them. What you want to address with change agents is the expected time and length of their participation. I was surprised to find that one of my clients had convinced a group of change agents to an indefinite term of service. That is an unusual expectation and, after several months, commitment began to fade. Most people can commit to an extracurricular activity outside their day-to-day job if it's well defined and within a reasonable amount of time. If the demands are high, you will have a hard time engaging the right participants, so it's important to have easy rules of engagement and make good use of their time.

When and How Do You Deploy Change Champions?

Let's consider the typical project management life cycle, which may include the following phases: initiation, planning, execution, monitoring, and closeout. The most optimal time to assemble and deploy a change champion group is during the planning phase of the initiative. By then, you would have created a structured approach of how the work will get done, and you may have information to share and feedback to gather.

The frequency of the change champion meetings depends on the rhythm of your organization. Most groups meet monthly or bimonthly, depending on the project duration. Clearly defining the role and expectations upfront will ensure that you gain momentum from the start.

How Do You Conduct a Change Champion Meeting?

Depending on the size of your organization, you may decide to schedule the change champion meetings in person or virtually. My preferred approach is to ask the participants to complete an online survey a few days prior to the meeting. With a few days to compile and analyze the data, I target the discussions around the pain points that surfaced throughout the surveys. During the meeting, I assign small-group discussions and collect the recommendations. I always present new information to the change champions and request that they circulate it within their spheres of influence. This open channel for feedback creates a loop where, collectively, we move the organization forward. Their feedback is escalated to leaders, and it is acknowledged. As appropriate, some of the input is put into action.

Agile Change Management

If you lead projects using the Agile methodology, change management activities, including the utilization of change champions, will be on a cyclical schedule. As the organization adapts to the mindsets and values of continuous improvement, change management becomes iterative and moves at a faster pace.

We used Agile change management on Rebecca's project for the insurance client I referenced earlier in this chapter. The remote work program was implemented through various waves. Each wave required a set of change management activities, which were repeated with the initiation of each wave.

The majority of the change-related work was finalized early in the project timeline, and then refined with the completion of each wave. Some activities, such as the Readiness Assessment, were completed once at the beginning of the initiative, while other activities, such as the various communications, were living documents on a schedule that required timely execution once they were created. Training was available just in time based on adult learning preferences. We tracked success measures with the expectation that metrics would improve with each wave.

Case for Change

Your change champions, and consequently all impacted stakeholders in your organization will want to understand the objective of the transformative work, or the Case for Change. This communication document may appear in multiple formats. Consider it the script that can be widely shared with leaders and change champions, so that the message is consistent and controlled. It addresses the most important questions on people's minds:

- What is this change?
- Why is this change important now?

- What will happen if nothing changes?
- Who will be impacted by this change?
- How will this change impact people?
- When will this change take place?
- What do I need to do now?

Drafting a Case for Change document requires a clear vision for the future. While some clients struggle to commit to a specific date, it is generally understood that an approximate date gives people a sense of timing so that they can prepare. The further out the date, the more understanding people are about the fact that something may potentially shift the timeline. A Case for Change document is foundational for future communications as it contains the essence of information about the transformation.

Awareness Campaign

At the base of your Awareness Campaign, which is the beginning of the communication activities, is the Case for Change information. As you launch your change champion network, you are essentially initiating the awareness campaign of your initiative. As a general guideline, people rarely keep secrets, so whatever is communicated to the change champions can be expected to echo consequently within the organization. Additional awareness campaign activities may include road shows, town hall meetings, department-specific gatherings, and broad, company-wide messages. When the awareness campaign launches, the project gains visibility and begins to gather momentum.

Conclusion

To move organizational change forward, we must invite people on the journey and empower them to lead in their sphere of influence. Something beautiful takes place when communication flows from within an organization and quenches the thirst of your people. Equip change champions with the appropriate sound bites, and they will carry the message further than you alone ever could.

KEY TAKEAWAY

Peer approval is a sign of multiplication. Leverage key influencers in your organization to magnify your message.

Consider the change you are leading and complete these action items:

☐ Go to marmonconsulting.com/no_ones_listening and download the Change Communication Strategy template.

☐ Identify ways to engage executive leaders throughout your organization.

☐ Identify ways to engage managers throughout your organization.

☐ Select key influencers within your organization to participate in a change champion network.

☐ Communicate the Case for Change within the change champion network.

☐ Complete the Channels section in the template.

CHAPTER 5

Turn on the Microphone

As we look ahead into the next century, leaders will be those who empower others.

—BILL GATES

In her book, *The Moment of Lift*, Melinda Gates describes the audacious vision of the Bill & Melinda Gates Foundation regarding controlling the global population and improving women's health. After several decades working with developing nations and collecting data through research, Melinda Gates and her colleagues were surprised to discover that the underlying reasons for the uncontrolled population were not only the lack of access to medical supplies but also deeply rooted, cultural implications that were in tension with the desired outcome for healthier communities.

In order to reach the most rural areas of the world, Gates deployed an army of native researchers with an organic approach to data collection. Using only a smartphone, the native researchers went to remote villages, knocked on doors, and asked women a set of specific questions. The data was richer and more meaningful than expected. In addition to responding to the questions, the women shared their stories, their struggles, and their pain. The sheer fact that someone cared to ask and listen was uplifting and encouraging to them, and it sparked a movement that is sweeping the world.

This series of events shows that Melinda Gates and her colleagues could achieve their audacious vision by establishing partnerships with existing nonprofits within the countries and influencing government officials through the discussion of policies. Achieving impact is not simply a question of financial resources. Achieving impact is accomplished by, through, and with strategic partners and local influencers who drive change in the cultural context of the ecosystem.

If you want to amplify your message, you need to turn up the volume.

Your MVPs

Much like the partnerships that the Bill & Melinda Gates Foundation leveraged, organizational influencers come in various forms, some with formal titles and prominent roles, and others with informal, less prominent roles. Identifying your organizational influencers is a critical component of leading change. In fact, it is one of the most important tasks you have as a leader.

In my experience of leading organizations through transformations, there is one stakeholder group that often does not receive the attention and communications it deserves, which, as a result, can derail the success of the change effort. This group is where most communications stop and never reach the intended front-line employees. It is the hardest stakeholder group to empower, support, and hold accountable due to the upstream and downstream demands.

Your most valuable players are your middle managers.

Does that surprise you? This group is often overlooked

because it's expected that they will follow the expectations of the executive team—yet, often, frustration exists on both sides. The managers are the closest influencers to the employees who are impacted by the change. The reason managers are a critical stakeholder group is because they directly impact your company operations, as well as your employees, who are the building blocks of your organization. Remember that before managers can serve in their managerial capacity, they are first and foremost employees. They experience the change curve just as any employee would, and they have unanswered questions while trying to address the questions of their teams.

A manager's ability to communicate with employees and their effectiveness to engage with their team is critical for many reasons. The neuroscience research of Dr. Judith E. Glaser confirms that the way we communicate releases physical and emotional changes in our brain.[4] According to Dr. Glaser, "Conversations have the power to change the brain by boosting the production of hormones and neurotransmitters that stimulate body systems and nerve pathways, change

---

4   Judith E. Glaser, "The Neuroscience of Conversations," *Psychology Today*, May 16,
      2019 https://www.psychologytoday.com/us/blog/conversational-intelligence/201905/
      the-neuroscience-conversations.

our body's chemistry, not just for a moment, but perhaps for a lifetime." Conversations steeped in trust can trigger "higher levels of dopamine, oxytocin, endorphins, and other biochemicals that give us a sense of well-being." Transactional conversations include an exchange of information that is asking and telling. Positional conversations require advocating and inquiring, where others can express opinions. Transformational conversations present leaders with the opportunity to cocreate conversations where sharing and discovering requires us to listen for deeper understanding. By engaging people in multidimensional dialogue, we establish trust, which is the foundational principle of leadership. Without trust, it is difficult to lead an individual to behave differently within an organization. Simply put, if people don't trust you, you can't lead them to transform.

Communication Messages

If you want to successfully lead change, provide managers with prescribed talking points about the transformation, and expect some variable of interpretation at their discretion. This can be accomplished in the format of frequently asked questions, manager town hall meetings, training sessions, videos, or other documents that can be leveraged by managers. The key is to provide them with repeatable sound bites for each stage of the initiative. Leverage the Case for Change document, which outlines answers to these managers' most critical questions.

Along with your change manager and the project team, decide what information middle managers need to receive in order to drive the change effort forward. To get you started, here is a list of potential topics:

1. Visionary message about the current state of your organization
2. How the transformation will impact your business, their work, and their teams
3. The urgency around timing and the duration for implementing the change effort
4. Desired outcome once the transformation has taken place
5. How the initiative integrates with existing organizational priorities
6. What is expected of managers for the success of the organization

The categories of information that managers are interested in knowing include the reason for the change, the approach to achieve the desired outcome, the schedule and timeline of what is ahead, the training that will be available to them and their employees, and the support model that will enable them to be successful. Sharing information with managers prior to dispersing the information throughout the organization ensures minimum surprises, since managers prefer not to learn of new strategic initiatives at the same time as their employees.

You need to tell them what you want them to say and when you want the information to be shared with the teams. Timing is everything. In his book, *When*, Daniel Pink highlights a study that discovered that our cognitive abilities vary throughout the day. People are more positive and optimistic in the morning, while their outlook on life takes a dip in the afternoon, and rises again in the early evening. Applying this finding to change initiatives suggests that, when communicating important information or critical decisions, it's optimal to do so in the morning rather than the afternoon.

I would also advise that you avoid communicating important information on Fridays, especially during the summer season when employees may be more prone to be out of the office or on vacation. Your objective is to minimize the probability that your messages would get buried in a pile of emails, or go unheard due to poor timing.

Remember my client, Rebecca, who was implementing the remote work program in chapter 3? Once we identified the critical role of the managers, we designed a change management approach to propel manager support and limit potential resistance. The managers received firsthand communication messages and check-ins from the sponsor as each wave was rolled out. They previewed content in advance and had an opportunity to provide input. We created customized presentations and specific messages they themselves were tasked to share. We established clear accountability through a monthly forum designed to offer them access to the leadership team, the HR business partners, and the project team. We put middle managers at the center of the change management efforts and empowered them to lead from within.

The key to successfully empowering managers is to establish a thorough support model. During the implementation of Rebecca's project, we offered a combination of formal and informal support throughout the duration of the initiative. With this particular client,

I recommended that our manager support model include four areas:

1. Change champion check-ins
2. IT support
3. Manager forum
4. Training, coaching, and communications

This blend of support ensured that managers could tackle challenges related to leadership engagement, technology, peer accountability, and performance management. Communicating the approach sent a clear message to the managers that they are not alone, and together we can achieve the desired objective and attract skilled talent.

We set the stage and turned on the microphone, but this time instead of the sponsor speaking, it was the managers who carried the message loud and clear in every direction within the organization.

We adjusted our approach based on their feedback. Our regular meetings provided insights into how managers needed to be supported. Since we deployed an Agile approach, we included a set of repeatable program surveys. With each wave, participating employees and managers received a survey at the completion of their wave. Curious about their experience, we asked about the program benefits, how it impacted the company culture, their ability to stay connected, perception around work recognition, and perception of career growth opportunities. The managers received additional questions around program benefits for the organization and their effectiveness in managing remote employees. The data gave the people a voice, and it helped us adjust and supplement our efforts to empower the people in their ability to redefine how and where they work.

Why We Don't Empower Others

Perhaps the most obvious reason why leaders miscalculate the importance of empowering others is because of the perceived loss of control. Power is not a zero-sum game. Influencers thrive in all levels of an organization, and they have earned the power given to them by their peers and leaders. Empowering influencers, managers, and partners to carry the mission forward yields progress that will benefit everyone.

When we give away power, it does not mean we have less of it; it means we make more of it through others.

How NASA Transformed through Partners

Most of us know NASA for its innovation and leadership in space technology, which was especially influential in the 1960s. NASA today is quite different—it's more diverse in its solutions, as well as its business model. According to a *Harvard Business Review* article, "The Reinvention of NASA," the organization "moved from being a hierarchical, closed system that develops its technologies internally, to an open network organization that embraces open innovation, agility, and collaboration."[5] This transformation forced the organization to evolve and adapt to its changing environment.

The challenge that NASA faced is familiar to many organizations: budget cuts. While its funding decreased, its vision increased. Government regulations, such as the Commercial Space Launch Act of 1984, required NASA to expand its reach into the commercial space. While commercial space organizations drove innovation in the low-earth orbit, NASA prioritized innovation into deep space. This called for collaboration and greater reliance on partnerships to accomplish its new mission. Change was inevitable.

---

5   "The Reinvention of NASA," by Loizos Heracleous, Douglas Terrier, and Steven
     Gonzalez, *Harvard Business Review*, April 23, 2018 https://hbr.org/2018/04/
     the-reinvention-of-nasa.

NASA approached the transformation by identifying three distinct phases that spanned over several decades, focusing on "technology strategies, cultural values, and ways of working with external parties." To be successful, NASA had to relinquish its control on how the contracted work was completed and how it engaged scientists from other space agencies around the world. NASA was forced to collaborate. To demonstrate its value and earn the American public's funding support, NASA invested more in external communications.

Its interactions with public organizations promoted shared technical responsibilities, which spilled into the consumer market. Partnerships, such as those with SpaceX and Orbital Sciences, shifted NASA's technology strategy, which resulted in shared costs and shared benefits across multiple industries. This cost-conscious approach has translated into innovation challenges targeting crowdsourcing solutions. NASA has become a more agile, collaborative organization poised for exploring new markets, both on Earth and beyond.

The shift in strategy forced NASA to relinquish its control and establish interdependent relationships with partners who could help carry the vision forward.

Conclusion

To achieve great impact, we must empower others to carry our vision forward. In your company, people of influence may be internal partners or external collaborators. Our diversity of perspectives and experiences provides engagement and a more collective and wholesome solution. And when we achieve our goals because of shared accountability, we all celebrate in the success of the mission.

Achieving success will most certainly require you to surrender control and embrace collaboration, inclusion, and shared accountability.

KEY TAKEAWAY

Equip managers with the talking points, offer adequate support, and unleash them to carry the message throughout the organization.

Consider the change you are leading and complete these action items:

☐ Go to marmonconsulting.com/no_ones_listening and download the Change Communication Strategy template.

- ☐ Identify which and how managers need to be engaged and supported.
- ☐ Provide managers with talking points and an action plan.
- ☐ Complete the Message section in the template.

PART 3

Speak

CHAPTER 6

—

Prepare the Stage

Communication works for those who work at it.

—JOHN POWELL

Ryan was an avid biker and showed up to every meeting full of energy. He was also a senior executive for one of my healthcare clients. Over the course of several decades, Ryan's company had grown to become a multisite specialty hospital chain across the United States, where each location operated independently along with competition and a hefty dose of comparison. As a result, each hospital had its own unique culture, its own operating structure, and its own job architecture. Then a new executive leadership came into place, and change was inevitable.

Ryan and I began working together on an HR system implementation project. This, however, came to a screeching halt when we realized that the various hospital locations had developed their own job titles and career structures as the organization grew organically. That had worked fine in the past, but the future of healthcare is constantly changing, and the urgency to be efficient was critical to the organization's success. Standardized job titles across all their hospitals were a must.

We knew this would be a tricky change. Job titles matter to people, and we wanted to demonstrate sensitivity to the individuals who were impacted by our project work. After all, we were wrestling with people's identities, and Ryan's ability to lead this transformation was a catalyst for other strategic initiatives related to technology implementations.

First, we set aside the HR system implementation initiative, as that was dependent on this more imminent job architecture work. We anticipated that the job title changes would impact up to 80 percent of the employees within my client's organization. This project was significant in scope because we reevaluated job salaries, qualifications, roles and responsibilities, and titles for all of my client's existing markets.

After months of behind-the-scenes assessments, interviews, discussions, and negotiations, we were ready to launch our communications. To decrease organizational tension and resistance, we communicated the components that would remain the same during job title transitions. This alleviated some of the uncertainty associated with the change, and positioned employees to openly engage in dialogue with their managers during the months ahead.

Communication Strategy

Crafting a communication strategy requires an understanding of how information flows within an organization. Skilled corporate communicators intentionally tap into the various communication channels to enable leaders to flow messages both top-down and bottom-up. These two different ways to distribute information provide an array of engagement opportunities along with easy-to-execute push communication strategies and intensive-yet-effective pull communication strategies. Examples of push communications include emails, newsletters, intranet articles, and other documents made available for people to access. Conversely, pull communications require discussions, focus groups, gatherings, and other forms of dialogue that necessitate interaction and active listening. In this chapter, we will explore the steps to create a communication strategy, communicate across generations, and apply a balanced mix of communication tactics to ensure that stakeholders have various opportunities to engage with the content and take action through participation.

Top-Down Approach

Most of us are familiar with a top-down approach of cascading information within an organization. As Patrick Lencioni writes in *The Advantage*, "There are three keys to cascading communication: message consistency from one leader to another, timeliness of delivery, and live, real-time communication." Cascading communications from the executive team ensure that there is consistency in the messages and that the information is synchronized throughout the organization. This requires coordination and precision of execution.

Due to the nature of the job architecture initiative that Ryan led, we cascaded messages from the top, starting with the CEO. To capture the essence of the message, we used video where the CEO introduced the job architecture work and explained how it contributed to the company-wide strategic goals and, ultimately, the success of the organization. He spoke empathetically and directly to the individual employees, addressed the "What's in it for me?" question, and asked for their commitment throughout the upcoming multitiered change initiatives.

This message triggered a set of communications to the directors, who then engaged the managers, who ultimately communicated to each person within the organization. It was like setting off a domino that triggered a set of reactions, seamlessly executing the orchestrated activities and ending in a grand finale. The messages were scheduled, positioned through the appropriate channels, and engaged individuals in respectful and transparent dialogue.

Bottom-Up Approach

Let's recall my client Karen, who worked at the non-profit with the audacious goals of changing the world in chapter 2. Karen was tasked to implement a new operating model; to do this, she leveraged a creative communication event. Since the work would impact the majority of the organization, the project team set up a booth during lunch so that most employees could participate. They held a "trash can'paign." Large trash cans were prominently displayed in the cafeteria, and employees were asked to write down everything they disliked about the current system. Papers were crumbled and thrown in the trash cans. While a sense of satisfaction flooded the participants, the project team eagerly collected the data and leveraged it to communicate how the future process would bring improvements. A little creativity can make a big impact when intentionally executed to stir up an emotional engagement and lead to action.

As you consider your organizational change initiative, how you flow information throughout your organization is incredibly important. Think of it as a synchronized dance, where each dancer moves in harmony, and all the dancers collectively create a mesmerizing and unforgettable experience.

Cascading communications is a majestic force that creates movement within an organization. The expectations are clear, precise, and timely. The execution is flawless. The results are on point. While this sounds idealistic, it is achievable with significant coordination and practice.

Communication Strategy Process

If you have been to London, you may be familiar with the London Underground, or Tube, transportation rail system. The Underground map contains lines, stations, and services for passengers to travel from one part of the city to another. While Harry Beck designed the initial map in 1931 to include only the Tube system, the most current map is inclusive of additional transportation options for passengers to create a comprehensive travel experience. If we were to study the Underground transportation system, we would identify traffic patterns, high travel times, number of passengers per day, and perhaps a variety of interesting information pertaining to the use of the transportation system.

Similar to the London Underground transportation system, in order to make an impactful movement of information within your organization, we must begin by identifying the existing communication channels. This important activity provides a map of the existing channels where information naturally flows. It is easier to leverage what is already in place than to create a new path where others have not been before. It is also optimal to make the most of existing meetings, forums, and technology to integrate your message within your organization.

As you begin this activity, think of it as a six-step process that starts out broad and narrows to formulate a refined strategy at the end. Communication is the lifeblood of an organization for connecting and exchanging information. Understanding the communication channels determines the type of messages used to achieve the intended impact.

Step 1

Identify all existing communication channels within your organization. Generate a list of all the options that come to mind, without intentionally eliminating channels that may not be used in your communication plan. Creating a broad list of options ensures that you don't overlook a potential communication opportunity. *Think of all the channels where information can flow.*

Step 2

Once all the communication channels have been identified, consider the audiences that are fed content through those channels. Each communication channel provides information to a specific audience group. *Think of the channels that are most frequently used.*

Step 3

Prioritize the communication channels where your messages will receive the most impact. Target specific communication channels where your highly impacted stakeholders typically reside. *Think of where your desired audiences naturally expect to receive content.*

Step 4

Identify the necessary frequency for your messages to be heard. In the case of communications, less is not more—more is more. People need to hear messages several times through various channels to understand them. *Think of the most optimal frequency and timing for your messages to be communicated.*

Step 5

Consider the sender of the messages. This is instrumental because it will determine if the message is received, how the message is interpreted, and what action the message drives. *Think about from whom the audience expects to receive the messages.*

Step 6

The final step of establishing a communication strategy is to consider the most appropriate frequency and timing of when the messages are to be distributed. *Think about the cadence when your intended audience can expect to receive new information.*

Once you have the initial communication channels planned, think of creative ways that can be leveraged to make a statement about your initiative. Most often, creative communications attract the most engagement and impact. They are sprinkled throughout the duration of the initiative, with an intentional outcome for each stage of the work.

As simple as these six steps appear, they require a level of intentional orchestration and thoughtfulness. Just like a skilled symphony conductor can detect specific instrument sounds, a savvy change leader can navigate the cultural norms, negotiate the integration of messages with existing communication channel owners, and influence the leaders so that the audiences are primed to receive the messages. The collective sounds echo throughout the organization with a rhythm and a beat that keeps the momentum propelling the organization forward.

Communications across Generations

It is no surprise that our communication styles must be tailored to resonate with our audience, specifically as we consider the various generations in the workforce. The technological advancements have pushed us to expect instant information and to have minimum patience for content that does not provide entertainment or immediate value.

According to The Center for Generational Kinetics, "The three key trends that shape generations are parenting, technology, and economics."[6] The philosophies

---

6   The Center for Generational Kinetics, https://genhq.com/annual-gen-z-research-study/.

we believe to be true shape our experiences. Each generation shares common perceptions about work and the meaning of life. It can be challenging to align every generation's core values to the organizational messages leaders send. To do so effectively, it requires intentional content creation to attract the attention of the desired audience, which is worth the investment of time and resources. Since organizations benefit from employees of diverse generational backgrounds, we can leverage various communication styles to ensure that all impacted stakeholders are engaged. Some prefer to keep the communications directive, while others prefer for the communications to be interactive, and yet some prefer the communications to be short. For example, while professionally staged video content may be best suited for the Baby Boomer generation, authentic personal videos appeal to Millennial and Gen Z audiences. This topic is important, and I recommend additional research to learn how best to relate and engage with each generation in your workforce, so that you can transform your organization.

Application in Action

Since we had crafted a seamless communication strategy, Ryan and his team at the hospital chain client that

I mentioned earlier executed their messages with ease. We hosted town hall meetings to prepare managers for the upcoming changes and to inform them prior to their employees receiving information. We had a plan for employees who might perceive a loss in status due to their job title change, and we had a special plan about how to help those individuals overcome resistance. The HR business partners were prepared to assist managers in handling difficult conversations.

This was a big shift within my client's culture, and we managed to execute it without significant turmoil. It was received well; people understood why it was important and how it would impact them. Some people left the organization, as we had expected, and those who chose to continue with their employment stabilized the organization as it embarked on the next change initiative. This turned out to be an elegant transition that could have been a devastating disaster.

Conclusion

Crafting a structured communication plan and executing it with intentionality and precision will ensure that your messages reach your intended audiences and empower your leaders as integral contributors to the success of the work. Understanding the way communications flow will enable you to tap into the pulse of your organization and strengthen its performance. Mastering the art of communication is the responsibility of every leader at every level within an organization. It is essential for the life of the organization.

KEY TAKEAWAY

A well-crafted communication strategy ensures that cascaded messages resonate at every level of the organization and reach the intended audience.

Consider the change you are leading and complete these action items:

- ☐ Go to marmonconsulting.com/no_ones_listening and download the Change Communication Strategy template.
- ☐ Identify the existing communication channels in your organization.
- ☐ Select the communication channels where your highly impacted stakeholders expect to receive information.
- ☐ Complete the Channel section in the template.

CHAPTER 7

─────

Cut Through the Noise

If you talk to a man in a language he understands, that goes to his head. If you talk to him in his language, that goes to his heart.

—NELSON MANDELA

"A farmer went out to sow his seed. As he was scattering the seed, some fell along the path, and the birds came and ate it up. Some fell on rocky places, where it did not have much soil. It sprang up quickly, because the soil was shallow. But when the sun came up, the plants were scorched, and they withered because they had no root. Other seed fell among thorns, which grew up and choked the plants. Still other seed fell on good soil, where it produced a crop—a hundred, sixty or thirty times what was sown" (Matthew 13:3–8).

For centuries, influential leaders like Jesus have been communicating through parables. These simple truths apply a storytelling technique to illustrate a deeply profound and vivid moral lesson. Jesus skillfully linked visual images of everyday life to spiritual foundations that were rich in meaning and rooted in cultural context. His ability to connect and relate to people drew crowds by the thousands, who eagerly longed for the words that dripped from his mouth. Regardless of our various spiritual beliefs, many of us are familiar with the parable of the Prodigal Son (Luke 15:11–32), or the Good Samaritan (Luke 10:29–37), or the Lost Sheep (Matthew 18:10–14). These stories carry a message that speaks to our core existence and our longing for wisdom, prosperity, purpose, connection, and a meaningful life. They challenge us to improve and enrich our existence through a transformative self-reflective invitation. These short stories are irresistible.

Today, stories continue to draw us in and captivate our attention. Whether through imagery or video, our brains are wired to look for patterns and decode meaning. Recently, my husband, Sam, and I took one of our sons to the local mall to spend special time with him. As we were walking to the nearby carousel, I was surprised to find my husband staring at a sign and looking intently at his phone. He was grinning, so I suspected something interesting caught his eye.

Sam ran over to show me codes on his phone, and I saw how excited he was to interpret a secret message. Someone was speaking his language! Sam is a computer and electrical engineer, and, at the time, we lived in a town known for attracting highly skilled engineers and scientists in droves. To me, the sign was invisible and irrelevant, but to Sam and his professional peers, it stirred curiosity and invited action. The sign had no contact information, no phone number, and no branding. It contained only a QR code and some obfuscated programming code.

What we must conclude is that those who are not your audience will ignore your message. To them, it will be completely invisible, so it's best not to waste efforts in putting out content that will not land on fertile soil. It is more important to spend time learning to address your true audience in their own language.

Decode Communications

Think of the language you use as the vibrations of radio waves. Radio waves have frequencies. Antennas receive transmitted radio waves. Relating this to communications, put out a frequency only in the band where your audience resides. When you transmit on the right radio frequency, your audience can tune in and receive your message loud and clear. Conversely, when you transmit on the wrong radio frequency, you are broadcasting static noise.

Cut through the noise by identifying the channels to which your audience is listening. Understand where they are getting their information from, and tune into their preferred channel with a message spoken in their language. A captivated audience can take action.

Similarly, when you communicate a message within your organization, keeping it broad, vague, and full of jargon typically equates to a message that is ignored. People listen for sounds they can interpret. If you speak to them in a foreign language they can't understand, you may catch their attention just long enough to realize they've moved on to something they can understand. Our bodies naturally want to preserve our brains from using too much brainpower. Simple messages are more memorable—they stick.

As you begin to communicate, build your message with

foundational content. Introductory messages answer the following questions:

- What is this about?
- What's in it for me?
- Why should I care?

As your work progresses, you can begin to insert layered messages where you touch on the foundational content and answer the following questions:

- How does it impact my work?
- What's expected of me?
- How does it align with our company vision?

As you sprint toward the finish line of your project, you will notice that peer approval becomes more important. People will want to see their managers and leaders demonstrate support and resonate with consistent messaging. Early resisters may then become more approachable. By then, the initial shock or excitement has morphed into the tactical execution of prescribed steps.

Visual Communications

While much of the communications are presented as

written content, visual communications are critical to convey the vision and progress of a change initiative. It is likely that most of your organizational communications are in the forms of emails, presentations, and meetings. It's important to encourage discussions and engagement with the impacted stakeholders, as the changes will force them to adjust their work.

Two visual communication mediums that I strongly encourage you to consider are videos and graphics. In my experience, videos are ideal to capture the executive sponsor's vision and ignite momentum within the organization. Periodic videos at key milestones present an opportunity to share progress. These videos can also be used for testimonials and small wins along the way to propel momentum. Videos are also a prime communication option for training and instructing, allowing individuals to pause and process information. As mentioned in the previous chapter, videos can captivate emerging generations and connect with individuals by presenting leaders through an authentic and genuine lens.

Visual communications also come in the form of graphics. This form of communication is beneficial to organizations that want to communicate progress, vision, and a path forward. Simplified messages through a branded campaign can provide a common language for people to gain insights on direction and what is ahead. Graphics can transform how your team members piece together their work with that of other teams for the purpose of collective progress. Graphics can also be deployed with a nimble approach at a smaller scale. Your visual communication strategy will be influenced by your organizational culture and the appropriate visual representation that helps individuals grasp the reason for the transformation.

The Power of Control

Do you want to be in control of your environment? If you lead any size of an organization, I am probably stating the obvious here, but hear me out on this one. This concept can transform how you communicate.

I had a revelation about control when I became a mother. In my case, becoming a mother required a season of waiting—then, within fifteen months, I was blessed to give birth to three children, and voila! I had an instant family.

As a parent, I quickly discovered how much was in my

control and just how much was not! I grew frustrated when timing and life circumstances worked against me, so like most driven people, I wrestled to get my way every chance I got.

My revelation about the power of control came to me through my children's daycare teacher. Ms. Nicole, who had exceptional parent-teacher communication skills, shared with me the importance of letting my toddlers find independence and their own voice. I remember standing in the middle of the daycare center that day, thinking about my work and the amount of control I wanted to have over people there, just as I wanted to control my toddlers. I had it all wrong. It wasn't my attempt to control others that got them to do what needed to be done. It was the amount of control I gave away that got people to take ownership and deliver.

We cannot manipulate people who are unwilling to do what we want, and we don't coerce people into action. That is unethical and unnecessary. Nothing can eliminate the uncomfortable but necessary conversations in order to address poor performance, dysfunctional team dynamics, and muddled expectations. It is your responsibility as a leader to initiate critical conversations with your people and mend working relationships where necessary, so that the organization can move forward with the change effort you lead. Giving away control invites others to become more accountable and find their voice throughout the change initiative.

Application in Action

In *Strategic Internal Communication*, David Cowan introduces the Dialogue Box, which is a communication model inclusive of five zones: intelligence, emotion, interpretation, narrative, and dialogue. In addition to the traditional model of communication channels and messaging, Cowan explores how audiences interpret communications according to how the messages relate to them. Leaders create a narrative that "like a story, has characters and a plot, with heroes (the leaders), villains (the competition, government), townsfolk (employees), and a love interest (customers)." The intelligence zone considers the decisions and leadership strategy required for the organization to change. The emotion zone considers employee response and reactions. The interpretation zone is the various points of view that exist in an organization. The narrative zone considers dominant and subdominant stories. Collectively, the zones entice a dialogue to "address power, opportunities, tensions, and conflicts."

By combining the planning of a traditional communication strategy, we can create a cohesive communication approach that engages people appropriately, addresses the potential resistance, and equips people to lead themselves and their organizations through change.

Conclusion

If speaking the language of your audience is instrumental to the success of your transformation efforts, consider the most optimal ways to reach people and help them see themselves as the heroes, rather than the spectators. To transform our behaviors, we must first see the world differently. We must see ourselves able to make decisions, influence our peers, and work toward a cause worthy of our time and efforts. We must see ourselves instrumental to the solution.

KEY TAKEAWAY

Speak the language of your audience. On the right radio wave frequency, you are not putting out noise; *you* are in tune with your audience, and you are communicating a message they expect to hear.

Consider the change you are leading and complete these action items:

☐ Go to marmonconsulting.com/no_ones_listening and download the Change Communication Strategy template.
☐ Complete the Story section of the template.
☐ How will people navigate the new landscape so they are the heroes, rather than the villains, in their story?

PART 4
———

Solve

CHAPTER 8

———

Say It Over and Over (Until It Works)

You can't manage what you can't measure.

—PETER DRUCKER

"I told them once—isn't that enough?" Christy asked during a private conversation with me. She seemed serious, so I looked her straight in the eye and said, "Say it again!"

Christy, who had great passion for her work, was implementing a new operating model for one of my insurance clients while introducing a new vendor partner, new technology, and a new hybrid claims management team at a new location. As the executive leader of the division, Christy intentionally angled to shift the organizational culture. This transformation was inevitable, based on the trends in the industry. Communicating with the impacted stakeholders and customers was instrumental in minimizing the level of disruption to the business, which we anticipated and proactively managed.

I get it—no one wants to sound like a broken record, especially intelligent, driven leaders with big visions and limited time. We tend to set a sporty pace. While we may have been training for this leadership marathon for decades, our people move at a different pace. Allow me to relieve your frustration and explain why.

In the early stages of my career, I found myself creating fancy spreadsheets with pivot tables, making catchy presentations with impressive data, and attending a multitude of meetings that often produced questionable value. Watching how leaders think fascinated me at a young age, and I found myself in close proximity to executives, perhaps out of pure curiosity on my part or their genuine interest to mentor me. While I exhorted my efforts to produce, produce, and produce, I realized that most of them hardly ever created something from scratch. They gave direction, they provided input, and they adjusted content, but rarely did they ever originate a document. As a leader, your value is not found in the quantity of work, but in the quality of thought.

Allow me to advocate on behalf of your people. Have you created a flurry of activities that keeps people preoccupied and distracted? Are they not listening, or is the environment you created cluttered? If that's the case, your people will not hear you the first time, or the second time, or the third time. Trust me. You've conditioned them to be busy, and busy is the enemy of productive. Busy people have no room for creativity, ingenuity, or space for delightful thinking and problem-solving. They can't hear your message. So yes, you need to say the message again.

Two Essential Conditions

While communicating the message is important, in my experience, organizations shift behaviors due to two favorable conditions. In order to achieve the desired results of the transformation you lead, consider how you model the new behaviors and align motivating incentives through the lens of communications.

The first condition is when people hear and observe their leaders demonstrate the desired behaviors. If you, as a leader, embrace the values of your organization, most people will naturally mirror your behavior.

I strongly believe that creating a strategy for the organization requires leadership insights and much finesse. Executing that strategy requires will and accountability. Similarly, leaders need to apply rigor when identifying organizational values and demonstrating desired behaviors. In the book, *Start with Why*, Simon Sinek explores the importance of understanding why organizations exist and what makes others attracted to their vision. Anyone who has invested time in strategic workshops to craft eloquent words to identify organizational values knows that it sounds easier than it actually is. Demonstrating the behaviors that align with the values is even harder. If we expect our people to embrace the organizational vision, our people expect us to demonstrate the way and guide them through the process.

The second condition is when incentives are aligned to encourage the desired behaviors. Unless there is a clear connection between the desired behaviors and how people are rewarded, appreciated, and recognized, it is difficult to change the way things have worked in the past. We conform toward the familiar in life.

One of my technology projects required highly skilled individuals to use a new system in a vastly different way. Industry regulations expected certain data to be captured in a specific manner. The project leader assigned to the initiative, Joe, was quite surprised when I asked to meet with the HR executive responsible for the incentive plan. After all, this was a data governance technology project, not an HR one! I assured Joe, who had managed complex programs for over a decade, that every aspect of the change strategy hinged on the organizational incentive model. Once I understood how and why people were recognized and rewarded for their work in the organization, I could validate if the new desired behavior would flourish or fail.

As you condition the organization for the change through modeling behaviors and aligning incentives, you can begin executing the communications accordingly. When you reflect on the sections of your Change Communication Strategy, complete the following:

- Identify the vision behind the work you are leading.
- Align within your organizational strategy.

- Obtain feedback from highly impacted stakeholders.
- Engage key influencers and leverage their people capital.
- Select communication channels with the most punch.
- Draft key messages to represent the various stages of the initiative.
- Craft a tailored story for each group.
- Identify and track KPIs to demonstrate progress.

Why We Don't Measure

While we know this is an important component of leading transformations, we don't measure results for several reasons. The most common reason is that we are unsure of what exactly to measure or how to obtain the data. Measuring results requires vulnerability. It's like anxiously looking into the mirror, which reflects the truth about our efforts. We also fail to measure our progress because we fear the outcomes.

Many clients struggle to identify and track metrics because they don't know what to track and how to gather the data. While managing organizational change may appear conceptual, I find it to be quite logical.

What to Measure

What do we measure? We measure the objectives behind the reason for the initiative within a reasonable time frame where we expect to see results. The full benefits of the initiative may not come to fruition until weeks, months, or perhaps years after the change is implemented. Identify and measure incremental milestones that support the objectives of the initiative.

For example, if we set out to retain valuable employees, we measure employee retention. If we set out to generate new business, we measure against profitability and new client acquisition. If we set out to merge two businesses and generate incremental revenue, we measure the outcome. It does not have to be complicated. Select a handful of important KPIs that will move your business forward.

How to Measure

When it comes to measuring change initiatives, the most effective way to tap into the people data is through surveys, feedback, and business statistics. Some organizations are survey saturated and prefer to tap into their change champion network for a pulse check with objective and subjective indicators. Regardless of the method, since we prioritize the shift in behavior, we can consider metrics that indicate progress.

When selecting the types of questions for a survey, ensure that there is a blend between numerical and open-ended options. While analyzing open-ended responses is time-consuming, it can be a window into the reality of how the initiative is impacting people. Some organizations offer surveys multiple times throughout the duration of the initiative. The questions may remain the same if the objective is to measure improvement over time. The questions may vary if the objective is to zoom in on particular challenges throughout the various stages of the initiative. Crafting questions that are not misleading will ensure that the data is objective and trustworthy. The key is to make the data accurate and actionable.

Consider ways to measure the effectiveness of your messages. There are some obvious statistics you can gather, such as the number of emails opened, links clicked, websites visited, questions asked, videos watched, and so on. The most important question to ask is, "Are you getting the desired benefits of the transformation?" If the communications are not yielding the desired results, they (along with perhaps other factors) are not effective.

Don't wait until the end of the transformation to track that. It will be irreversibly too late.

Why It Matters

Collecting data for the sake of data collecting is wasteful. Rather, you should distribute the data from those who could benefit from it. Use it to make informed decisions and shift direction. If your messages are ineffective, apply a different strategy. If your managers are not engaged, entrust them with more ownership. If the undercurrents of your industry shift, change the initiative. Data is important to people. It requires a give-and-take exchange, and those who provide feedback also expect action. You are not required to act upon every suggestion, but you must acknowledge the feedback. If you fail to do so, the feedback will cease and it will be only your voice that fills the void.

Sometimes the unfortunate happens, and, halfway through the project work, leaders realize something is not working. I have seen my clients wrestle with this, and it is difficult for everyone. The hardest and bravest thing to do is pause the work, reevaluate, and adjust the decision. It's likely that your people are wrestling with the challenge as well, and if you communicate the reason behind the change in strategy, they will understand.

We collect data to make informed decisions, and yet, data is often hoarded or misinterpreted. Inquire about who needs access to the information and why. Who will support the work due to the data? Who will use the data to encourage others? Who will change their approach in light of the data? What you present and how much of it you present matters. How the data is presented is of significance to the people responsible for taking action.

Celebrate!

If you thought all roads lead to metrics, you were wrong. In an ideal situation, all metrics lead to celebrations. This is the most frequently omitted communication regarding large initiatives. We may see a glimpse of it at the beginning when the work begins and the excitement is high, but by the finish line, it has dwindled away. Why?

The reason it disappears is because most significant transformations rarely go as planned. They are not on budget, they are not on schedule, and they don't yield the desired results in the unreasonable amount of time we expect to see progress. Self-conscious, bright, and driven leaders consider their work—and, by default, the work of their teams—as undeserving of recognition. This is unfair. While the luster and excitement may have vanished, your people have invested much to reach the end of the tunnel where there is light!

Now is the time to celebrate and recognize the accomplishments that worked. To be celebrated indicates private and public affirmations for our contributions. Shine a light on the people who made it happen. Raise a toast to overcoming challenges, conquering obstacles, and climbing out of ditches. Show kindness to others, and to yourself, for learning new skills, demonstrating endurance, and stretching beyond the comfort of the everyday ways of work.

Conclusion

As we conclude this last chapter of the book, cheers to you, my dear leader. Your sweat and tears may be unnoticed by most, but I've seen your perseverance and unbreakable will, your sacrifice, and your relentless drive. May your celebration be of who you've become, not simply your achievements. May you delight in the abundant impact you've generously imparted on others. May you bask in the glory of deep connections with people who will forever be transformed by you, and you likewise by them. May you confidently transform your organization and positively impact the world.

So stand boldly in the face of change, in the turbulence of uncertainty and fear, at the bottom of the valley of despair, and at the mountaintop of the adventure. And remember—you've got this!

What's Next?

On our website, marmonconsulting.com, we offer various free resources, such as videos and checklists, that provide you with valuable advice as you lead your organization through change. Grab the free resources, check out our articles, and if you'd like to have a further discussion about how our team can help you achieve successful change outcomes, we would love to connect. Our services require a conversation to provide us insights into your situation so we can best serve you. We offer customized workshops, Readiness Assessments, and structured change management engagements for your transformational initiatives. Want to learn more? Connect with us at hello@marmonconsulting.com.

Consider the change you are leading and complete
these action items:

- ☐ Go to marmonconsulting.com/no_ones_listening
  and download the Change Communication Strat-
  egy template.
- ☐ Complete the Metrics section of the template.
- ☐ How will you measure progress?
- ☐ How will you acknowledge and celebrate success?

Conclusion

Return to Me

"How do you know if the transformations you lead last over time?"

It was a valid question and one that is difficult to address in front of an audience of unfamiliar faces. I gripped the microphone and felt uncomfortable about the response I really wanted to give—which was, "I don't know."

I was speaking at a conference for nonprofit organizations and had unloaded insights on how to lead transformations. Their hunger for change fueled me to give them what I had learned from my clients on the commercial side.

My response to the question sounded more like this: "As a consultant, I don't have the privilege to track how changes unfold once I transition out of the organization. I encourage the leaders to keep the drumbeat going, monitor behavior, adjust incentives, and communicate." It was inadequate, and I knew it. It pains me that consultants feel this way.

After the presentation was finished, Eric, the gentleman who asked the question during my presentation, continued the conversation with me. A woman, Liz, stepped up and inserted a comment that shocked me. Liz said, "I know who your client is."

I had opened my presentation with a story about a Seattle client that was undergoing a transformation around strategy, technology, and culture. I protect the identity of my clients and don't disclose their names, so it took me by surprise when Liz assertively named the organization and proceeded to tell me what followed. She shook my hand and said that, eight years ago, when I transitioned out of the client, she entered as an employee, now working remotely halfway across the United States. She said, "Thank you for your work. I can tell you confidently that your work made a difference and improved how we work as an organization."

The three of us stood there in a moment of disbelief. His question, her response, and my longing to make a difference intersected all at once. For all the failures we face in this field of managing change, moments like these breathe in hope, a confirmation that this work is worth something grander than our collective efforts. It makes a difference.

Now that we have explored the acronym LESS (listen, empower, speak, solve), you can confidently move forward with planning and executing your change initiatives. When you pause to listen and empower others more, you allow your people to speak and share the messages, so that everyone participates in solving, achieving, and celebrating the success.

Shall we journey into the future? Imagine that day when it is you standing at that podium again, gripping its sides and leaning forward with enthusiasm.

Your presentation is polished, the stage is set, and you are ready for the big announcement. The chairs are in perfect rows, one behind the other, empty and cold—for now.

You sift through your notes, palms sweating, yet you are

confident because this is not your first time persuading a crowd. This is a message they have been anticipating. This message will change their future.

But this time, they helped you refine the vision, craft the message, rally enthusiasm, and bring others along. They *want* to embrace the future with all the mysteries it holds. They are ready.

You go through the message. There was plenty of time to rehearse it because it has already been echoing through your organization. You take a deep breath. You were never alone.

People are filling the room one by one, coffee in hand. You overhear chatter in the background. You smile, and on the inside, you feel giddy with excitement. They sense your joyful emotions as you radiate a genuine enthusiasm to be in the moment.

You are an accomplished leader, vested in their success, and yours. You care deeply about the company's future. You care deeply about the people.

The time has arrived. The microphone is turned on. You hear your footsteps as you walk up to the podium and clear your throat. You toss the notes aside and speak from your heart. The bright lights are not on you this time; they are on the employees, shining their support.

Their voices echo through the room.

You hear a cheer, some clapping. You hear yourself laugh with joy. You hear them return that giddy, happy laughter. You pause and bask in the moment. There is silence.

Everyone is listening…and it's your fault.

Acknowledgments

Back in 2005, when I graduated from Calvin University with my undergraduate degree, I wrote down a list of lofty dreams, one of which was to author a book. At the time, I didn't have the words or the insights to know how the book would impact the world. I am grateful for the time and all my experiences, both the positive and the deeply painful ones, which have contributed to my professional and personal growth. Before any of them existed, God knew my journey. I am first and foremost thankful for Jesus' sacrifice on the cross. He gives my life a purpose.

This book would not be possible without the continuous encouragement of my husband, Sam Marmon, who spent many nights putting our kids to bed while

I wrote in quiet. He has given my dreams wings to fly, and I am forever grateful for his love. My parents, Ivanka and Dinko Haralakovi, and my sister, Rosie Diedrich, have cheered me on as I set out to chase many new adventures. Words cannot describe how grateful I am for the many lessons they have taught me. I am who I am because of them. Their perseverance and hard work are forever etched in my soul.

While writing this book, my dear friends Irina Beckner, Rachel Jolokai, and Kiera Ojo spent countless hours sharing feedback, perspective, and encouragement. I will always remember their kindness to me. A huge thanks to my book-launching team filled with many beloved friends, mentors, and peers, who believed I could author a book and helped me embrace my new identity as a writer. I am forever grateful for everything I've learned from my professional colleagues, who have coached and mentored me to become who I am today. I am a better consultant because of you.

This book couldn't be possible without Tucker Max, Hal Clifford, Tashan Mehta, the Scribe publishing team, and Cynthia Moll. Your work is magic! Thank you for teaching me how to author a book. I couldn't have done it without you.

To all my remarkable mentors, Shirley Hoogstra, Mary Devon, Andy DeVries, and Stacy Jackson, who coached me on how to get up when I got knocked down and how to dream big, thank you! To my pastors, who taught me the power of God's redemptive love, thank you! To all my students, current, past, and future, who inspire me to believe in a brighter tomorrow, thank you! To all my clients—you know your true identity, though it is hidden on these pages. Walking with you is my life's real joy. You are my true heroes. You make my work rich and fulfilling. Thank you!

To you, my dear reader, who shares the desire to transform your organization—this book would be nothing without you. This book is for you. Thank you from the bottom of my heart. Be the change catalyst our world needs!

About the Author

PAM MARMON is the CEO of Marmon Consulting, a change management consulting firm that provides strategy and execution services to help companies transform. From Fortune 50 to startups, Pam brings unparalleled change expertise and insights as a practitioner, a speaker, and an adjunct professor of future change-makers. Growing up in Bulgaria and moving to America has taught her to be adaptable and resilient to change. Pam and her family live in Nashville.

References

Cowan, David. *Strategic Internal Communication: How to Build Employee Engagement and Performance*. Philadelphia: Kogan Page, 2014.

Creasey, Timothy J., and Stise, Robert. *Best Practices in Change Management*, 9th ed. Loveland, CO: Prosci Research, 2016.

Gates, Melinda. *The Moment of Lift: How Empowering Women Changes the World*. New York: Flatiron Books, 2019.

Glaser, Judith E. "The Neuroscience of Conversations: A Deep Dive into the Fascinating World of Conversations" *Psychology Today*, May 16, 2019. www.psychologytoday.com/us/blog/conversational-intelligence/201905/the-neuroscience-conversations.

Gray, Brad. "Jesus and His Explosive Parables" Walking the Text. Video, accessed October 24, 2019. www.walkingthetext.com/episode-081-jesus-and-his-explosive-parables/.

Hiatt, Jeffrey M., and Creasey, Timothy J. *Change Management: The People Side of Change*. Loveland, CO: Prosci Research, 2003.

Kotter, John P. *Leading Change*. Watertown, MA: Harvard Business Review Press, 2012.

Lencioni, Patrick. *The Advantage: Why Organizational Health Trumps Everything Else in Business*. Jossey-Bass: Wiley Imprint, 2012.

Lewis, Alan, and Dan McKone. "So Many M&A Deals Fail Because Companies Overlook This Simple Strategy" *Harvard Business Review*, May 10, 2016. www.hbr.org/2016/05/so-many-ma-deals-fail-because-companies-overlook-this-simple-strategy.

Maurer, Rick. *Beyond the Wall of Resistance: Unconventional Strategies that Build Support for Change*. Austin: Bard Books, 1996.

Maurer, Rick. *Beyond the Wall of Resistance: Why 70% of All Changes Still Fail—and What You Can Do About It*. Austin: Bard Press, 2010.

Miller, Donald. *Building a StoryBrand: Clarify Your Message So Customers Will Listen*. New York: HarperCollins Leadership, 2017.

Pink, Daniel H. *When: The Scientific Secrets of Perfect Timing*. Melbourne: The Text Publishing Company, 2018.

Prosci. Change Management and Agile Report. Accessed August 28, 2019. www.prosci.com/agile.

Sinek, Simon. *Start with Why: How Great Leaders Inspire Everyone to Take Action*. London: Penguin, 2009.

Tasler, Nick. *Ricochet: What to Do When Change Happens to You.* Edina, MN: Beavers Pond Press, 2017.

Heracleous, Loizos *et al.* "The Reinvention of NASA" *Harvard Business Review*, April 23, 2018. www.hbr.org/2018/04/the-reinvention-of-nasa.